AGOG

PETE MARSHALL

CinnamonPress

INDEPENDENT INNOVATIVE INTERNATIONAL

Published by Cinnamon Press
Meirion House
Glan yr afon
Tanygrisiau
Blaenau Ffestiniog
Gwynedd, LL41 3SU
www.cinnamonpress.com

British Library Cataloguing in Publication Data. A CIP record for
this book can be obtained from the British Library.

Designed and typeset in Palatino by Cinnamon Press.
Cover from original artwork 'View from Cwm Idwal' by Bridget
Jones © Bridget Jones, agency dreamstime and detail from Welsh
map © Ordance Survey, used with permission.
Cover design by Cottia Fortune-Wood.

Printed in Poland

Cinnamon Press is represented in the UK by Inpress Ltd
www.inpressbooks.co.uk and in Wales by the Welsh Books
Council www.cllc.org.uk.

The publisher acknowledges the support of the Welsh Books
Council

Acknowledgements

Some of these poems first appeared in *Poetry Wales, The New Welsh Review, Envoi* and *Kaleidoscope*, an anthology of poetry sequences published by Cinnamon Press.

The author would like to thank Avid Publications for permission to use material appearing in this collection. Thanks also to Snowdonia National Park for permission to use material from its website. Thanks to Plaid Cymru for permission to use Gwynfor Evan's Tryweryn letter. And many thanks to the University of Wales Press for permission to use material from its publication *The Holy Wells of Wales*. The Welsh map poem is published under Ordnance Survey license.

Many thanks to Sion and Gwen for their kind assistance with this project.

Thanks to my mum, Glenys Mair, for the Welsh blood and heritage and cheers Dad for invoking the majesty and magic of Snowdonia when we were very young.

Finally, and most importantly, thanks to my beautiful wife, the love of my life, for everything.

Contents

a bright star 9

diamond cut 10

Picture Poem 1 – Wells 1 11

Cerrigydrudion 12

tombstone waymarker 14

a debate initially sedate 16

John 18

Beddgelert 19

incongruous 22

The indiscriminate transfer 24

The Roman road 25

Carneddau Spring 26

Water is the first element 28

Picture Poem 2 – Taffy 29

…and sometimes 30

I use sacred water 31

in Betws Y Coed 32

Goronwy ap Dewi 33

Nain and Taid come to tea 36

Before Port Dinorwic became Y Felinheli 38

Picture Poem 3 – Wells 2 39

…and the American kept saying 40

[Pete the Poet… 41

trail 42

…see beautiful Gwenno 43

Mach 1 44

Llangelynnin 45

On composite principalities 46

on a bootlace of black-top 47

to kill and skin 48

Picture Poem 4 – Map of Wales detail 50

…I'll tell you what ol' son 51

I use one ancient ritual   56
Nant Peris   57
Stan Taylor / Jimmy Callaghan   58
Legend has it   59
Picture Poem 5 –
    a debate initially sedate 2/Rhododendron   60
Beech Plantation Rowen   61
I know that well water   62
curl of woodsmoke   63
little Gwenno   64
Picture Poem 6 – Letter to PM, 1957   65
A medicine sister   66
...at the Urdd Eisteddfod   67
frontiersville   68
Picture poem 7 – 'A generall Bill', 1665   70
after the cut   71
I am a direct descendant   72
Pen y Gaer   73
at the wall's   74
[...Pete the fuckin' Poet...   75
the view lies   76
under the lake   78

For Matthew,
who loved the mountains,
see you up there Bro

AGOG

A bright star rises above a stable on a traditional Welsh hill farm on the outskirts of Capel Garmon. Strangers from away arrive. With pressies. A baby cries. The stable door opens and a farmer, whose trousers are held up with baling twine, enters. "I don't bloody care who you are," he says, "I'll be lambing in here tomorrow so you can bugger off."

[*Trad, Anon.*]

diamond cut
pink Penderyn sky

slow helix of grey smoke

Siop Y Foel cupped
in the hand of the hill;

between gaps
in the herringboned wall

a stiletto wind
stabs the silver cob's flank;

stark black
against feathered pine

gabled walls, lintelled windows,

empty spaces;

and at the Welsh knight's grave
hoar breath plumes

a gauntlet of hazel fingers
grips the frozen land

one purpled metacarpal
points north

Questions for ▮▮▮

1/. Could you comment briefly on the enclosed papers.

2/. I have seen offerings (cloth, pins, coins etc) at wells. Have you ever use well water for purification purposes, or for any other reason in your work?

3/. Do you feel that wells, or the water in them, might still have healing properties?

4/. Could you describe any purification, or cleansing ritual you use in connection with your work or belief?

5/. Do you ever visit wells?

6/. Do you ever visit standing stones, cromlechs, or stone circles in connection with your work or belief?

7/. Do you use feathers, herbs, bones or stones in your work or in the practise of your belief?

8/. What does Welsh water mean to you? Does it have power?

9/. Do you know anybody, or have heard of anybody, of an older Welsh generation who used, or spoke of, or had some knowledge the old ways of healing?

Just a few wells my father visits!

- Ffynon Penrhyn - pistyll y Llan - Sbyty Ifan the acid apparently.
- Ffynon Eidda - Ar y migneint (at the site Byd Joeboicier anti depressed? old tavern on the old be Thankful. drovers' road).
- Ffynon ty Nant - ?onglybeate Sulphur & ? Calibeate well, above Ysbyth Ifan, people would come from afar with offerings, there would be seats and cups left for travelers. A friend of my father's had a terribly painfull shoulder for a long time and decided to place his arm up to his neck in this well (same well as the one my father took me to for healing as earlier mentioned) this he did twice with amazingly rapid results and full freedom from pain that lasted - but he never had shoulder problem again. Anaemia, rheumatism, arthritis, depression

Ffrayn Penymladdfa - also above Ysbyty Ifan - would spend hours as a child ogying nd playing at this well.

Ffynon Jiwbili Victoria - outskirts of Sbyty no water → overgrown!

11

Cerrigydrudion

drizzle immemorial
drew me back to scratch the prodigal itch.
Chingachgook remains,
older now, passive,
chromium mount
tethered to pitting asphalt.

The rasher's smile
still bleeds ketchup,
while cook thumbs ants
on curling Formica.
Elvis lives
in the Tardis,
but croons a different tune.

Birchbark savages ooze
yellow as yolk
onto my plate,
and I can almost hear
the crackle of pine musketry,
smell his old Holborn cardy,
visualize her madness
dancing with the dust

but the images sting
like slapped legs.

Outside foxgloves wave:
love letters in the sand
warp by the pig-bin's peel,
the urinals reek
and seem to bubble burdock,
sacrificial longlegs
dangle hideously
from greying webs.

Our heraldic runes,
carved so many years before,
remain in slate.
Porcelain towns,
no mystery now,
brown sadly in china.

Opal fruits
and ice cream;
I leave the place haunted,
glancing back
like an infant
fleeing from the dark.

tombstone waymarker
fog and mist and cloud
[*zero visibility*]
alone and lost

tangible
      echoes
            muffle

the sound of distant water flowing;

      on the Migneint
the Tylwyth Teg play the otherworld shuffle
      turn things upside down

light will-o-the-wisp candles
in the spectral portals of sham cottages

make this spongy bogland path feel safer
      somehow

      familiar
as the smell of an old collie's blanket;

      I'm frightened;

not far away a woman stifles a giggle
      a man coughs

much further out the clatter
of iron shoes on
cobblestones

      a horse blows

the creak of a leather harness
    the jangle of a bit
        the crack of a whip

and the wooden groan of a wagon's slow approach;

next morning when the sun rises
over the snow-capped peak of Arennig Fach
to burn the fog from the moor

pooled cauldrons of mist form in the valley;

in the part frozen Conwy lake
a sickle mooned reflection

an inverted horseshoe of Glyder hills;

it's mid-January and still the midges rise

a debate initially sedate

the poet speaks

> *personally I dislike all forms of Nationalism; I believe it to be*
> *narrow, divisive, xenophobic, exclusive racism that in its*
> *higher form allows normally civilised and cultured people to*
> *throw other people into gas chambers*

Strongbow over ice, pork belly in hoisin, Wolfblass and
later after the ladies have retired a bottle of finest Penderyn
Welsh whiskey in the conservatory

the bard speaks

> *my god yes I despised them, hated them all, to me they were a*
> *plague, an infection poisoning the blood of my culture; how*
> *many times I drew a bead on that bloody usurper, that foreign*
> *prince, the iron sites of my father's old 303 Lee Enfield rifle*
> *set in the middle of his face, and I could have done it too by*
> *god I could, from the hills above Betws, yes and got away*
> *with it. And I regret now not pulling the trigger, but by god*
> *how I rejoiced every time the IRA killed an English soldier*
> *and by god how I celebrated the death of Mountbatten his*
> *own German blood sullied and thinned and spoiled by the*
> *bloody poisonous English*

the lad serves

a bottle of Wild Turkey

the bard goes on

> *of course we were colonised boy, we're still fuckin' colonised*
> *by god the English plague has infected our blood forever and*
> *the sop or gift of our own language is nothing more than a*
> *poisoned chalice*

the bard stands

lurches forward, performs an ungainly pirouette, followed
by a flailing headlong dive into a coffee table full of used
glasses and a vase of freshly cut daffodils

the lad enquires as to his well-being

the bard concludes

*naaar boy I'm fuckin' drunk as fuck, is there any more
whiskey lad, and don't go bombing Iran boy, it's the cradle of
fuckin' civilisation for fuck's sake*

John, a prim and bitter teacher,
changes his name to

IOAN AP DAFYDD

moves to Penrhyndeudraeth
for the length of the name
and the anonymity,
returns to Wrexham weekends
for his Mam's roast lamb dinners
and to criticise his father for

speaking that bloody common
Rhos Welsh

Beddgelert

1

mariner's chests packed with trove
slung aloft and lashed under oiled tarps

our prairie schooner
a mini traveller

on single track lanes
with no passing places

in the forest

Cyffylliog
Clocaenog

crossroads
signposts

and over the moor

the picnic place
the fishing place

the caff at Cerrig

and in the back
three boys under sheepskins

rolled with the bends
the hairpins at Padog

glimpsed lights at night on the dark hills

whispered tales of wizards
warlocks and witches

forgotten children
left lost and lonely by sad parents

to dwell in caves in fur

to forage in the Welsh wilds
with the tigers and the coughing rams

2

smell of
methylated spirits
warm egg sarnies
Welsh blankets
Heinz Tomato Soup

it never rained because
it was always summer

I remember
lying on bunny bullets
on tufty grass
next to the river
hands behind my head

cloud counting

riding the unicorn
in the ruins

watching the copper fox
cross the mountain

feeling sponge earth
shrink beneath me

and under the bridge
learning to swim

trout in the weed
against the skin

in heavy water
a light hand
on a soft belly

incongruous
against a pristine alpine backdrop;

chippy wrappers
crushed fag packets
generic lager cans
disembowelled kebabs
take away cartons
styrofoam cups

skidder of twice trod
anaemic dog shit

in charity shop windows
flyers beckon

learn Welsh
Tai Chi for beginners
African drumming tonight

and on the Spar's wall
hand painted in lurid green
and aerosoled pink

Gwenno is a fat slag
English out
MUFC forever
Bryn Jones sucks cocks
Cymru nid ar werth

leaving the village
a glance in the rear view reveals

a local wag's scrawled calligraphy

CROESO
BETHESDA
WELCOME
[*Twinned with Beirut*]

The indiscriminate transfer of English people into Wales will place the Welsh language, and even the very existence of the Welsh nation, in jeopardy. The national welfare of the Welsh people should be a matter of first consideration by the authorities who are planning evacuation into our countryside. We, as Nationalists, demand that there should be no transfer of population into Wales that would endanger Welsh Nationality. If England cannot make its emergency plans without imperilling the life of our little nation let England renounce war and grant us self-government.

To treat Wales merely as an English 'reception area,' to the evident endangerment of all Welsh social tradition and social unity, is to show towards Wales a spirit of militaristic totalitarianism contrary to all principles of democracy and to the rights of small nations.

the Roman road

a blizzardy wind

under snow
water flows
turf
sod and soil
cobblestoned
sub-strata

antediluvian foundations
layered millennia

out of the white-out
Caer Bach
homesteads
Maen Y Bardd dolmen
the dwarfstone circle
Swan Inn ruin

and at
Bwylch Y Ddeufaen
stones loom
under hissing cables
hum
like transformers

behind us
footprints follow

outlanders
pass through

settle in

Carneddau Spring

pashmeena woodsmoke
on the greening hill

between two towns
the river
slowspoolsbendscurves
gentle as an arm
around the shoulder
of an old friend

beneath hung steel
freshwater pebbles

shaped
watersmooth
Conwy bluegrey
and warmed in the sun
once dipped
shed quickdried
mercurial bubbles
like hot oil
in a cottage skillet

and in the shallows
perfect
jet black
and polished ebony
sleek and otterslick

and in her palm
snug
as a memory
of a shoulder ride
on a sealskin beach
where reluctant stones
left her hand
to skim
hissing
far away
long ago last summer

Water is the first element according to the ancient philosophy 'the mother of all things (mam ni oll)' water gave birth to spirit, supposedly a masculine principle, hence the idea of baptismal re-birth that the Christians copied from pagan worship which involved both water (feminine) and spirit (masculine.)

Springs, fountains, ponds and wells were always female symbols in archaic religions, their powers were used in sacred and holy healings. Many pagan sacred springs and wells throughout Wales were thought to have serpents, eels or vipers living in, or close, to them...snakes also being associated with the female principle of a wom-b-man's energy, this being a serpent which lies curled in the womb of a woman until such time that, as the woman evolves spiritually when the serpent awakes and reaches up though her centres and into her third eye, place of psychic energy, wisdom, enlightenment (a woman's intuition.)

Guardians or keepers of this goddess energy within the sacred places were said to be water deities or elemental spirits, their healing powers differed from well to well, depending upon which deity guarded the place. It is to these guardians that offerings are made as energy exchange for the healing received.

Wells are also water passages to the underground womb of the great mother (earth) a place to access other realms. Their magic water is used in divination or to cast spells.

St Mary's priory, near Dinas Moch, Beddgelert, has 'Llawer o rinweddau swyngyfareddol' or many healing virtues. This is the female principle of the sacred places, they are the water wombs of mother earth, places of hugely condensed earthly power which when respected and honoured in the old ways can be magical, healing and life giving.

[*Taffy was a Welshman Taffy was a thief Taffy came to my house and stole a piece of beef I went to Taffy's house Taffy wasn't home Taffy came to my house and stole a marrow-bone I went to Taffy's house Taffy was in bed I took the marrow-bone and beat about his head*]

about his head Taffy was a Welshman Taffy was a thief Taffy came to
stole a piece of beef I went to Taffy's house Taffy wasn't home Taffy ca
e and stole a marrow-bone I went to house Taffy was in bed I
ow-bone and beat about his head Taffy was a Welshman Taffy was a th
to my house and stole a piece of beef I went to Taffy's house Taffy was

According to Green this song was, "Sung in derision along the Welsh borders on St. David's Day. Formerly it was the custom of the London mob on this day to dress up a guy and carry him round the principal thoroughfares. The ragged urchins following sang the rhyme of 'Taffy was a wicked Welshman'."

use and a marrow-bone I went to Taffy's house Taffy was in bed I took
arrow-bone and beat about his head was a Welshman Taffy was a thief Ta
me to my house and stole a piece of went to Taffy's house Taffy ho
iffy came to my house and stole a marrow-bone I went to Taffy's house Taffy v
bed I took the marrow-bone and beat about his head Taffy was a Welshman Ta

v-bone I went to Taffy's Taffy was in bed I took the marrow-bone a
out his head Taffy was a Welshman Taffy was a thief Taffy came to my ho
le a piece of beef I went to Taffy's house Taffy wasn't home came to
and stole a marrow-bone I went to Taffy's house Taffy wa I took
v-bone and beat about his head Taffy was a Welshman Taffy was a thief T
b my house and stole a piece of beef I went to Taffy's house Taffy wasn't ho
came to my house and stole a marrow-bone I went to Taffy's house Taffy

the 17th and 18th centuries, it was common in England to use the verb 'Welsh' to imply thievery or dishonesty — to 'Welsh' on a deal — or the adjective 'Welsh' to mean inferior quality or an outright counterfeit. In an age where practically everyone knew how to snare a rabbit for the pot, a Welshman was considered to be so lazy and inept that snaring a rabbit for the pot was beyond him. Cheese and bread had to do instead

to Taffy's house Taffy wasn't home came use and
w-bone I went to Taffy's house Taffy in bed I arrow-b
out his head Taffy was a Welshman as a thief Taffy came to m
le a beef I went to Taffy's house Taffy wasn't home cam
and stole a marrow-bone I went to Taffy's house Taffy wa I t
v-bone and beat about his head Taffy was a Welshman Taffy was a thie
b my house and stole a piece o went to Taffy's house Taffy wasn
came to my house and stole a marrow-bone I went to Taffy's house Ta

...and sometimes at the end of a blind cwm where the black cloud is held low and shroud-like year round by a horseshoe of dark hills and the thunder echoes drummish against the rock and the grim lake swallows up the endless rain a man can watch three generations of the same family die in the same squat cottage the wind hammering at the doors of his sanity the fluke and the damp and the mould that took grandparents and parents and brothers alike leaving him with the weight of the world on his shoulders and the smell of the bog on his skin and God's biblical plagues of frog and fly and maggot and rotting white corpses pressing relentlessly upon his childlike humanity his yellow nails trimmed when they curl with sheers and his toothless jabber monotonous and long ago giving up on the journey to town or store or market now existing only on mutton or lamb cooked or otherwise and watching [*a lonely simian soul*] from the dank ffridd and cold barn the comings and goings of the shining girls with their tight clothes and golden hair swaying from side to side like the tails of beautiful ponies as they walk, watching with an acquisitive magpie's eye and wondering aloud to himself if he could keep just one just for a little while just one just for a little while...

I use sacred water in my healing work. I make an offer prior to using it. I do not always get permission to take the water and sometimes have to leave it. I utilize my role as healer to cleanse or purify auras (our energy field or spirit body.)

I have also used water (as I would sage smoke) to cleanse and protect my own aura and hands prior to healing (in much the same way as a surgeon scrubbing up prior to an operation.)

in Betws Y Coed
a Manc charabanc
slowly disgorges
cotton-topped grockles

from a park bench
Dai Slate enjoys

the divine comedy
of scowling brothers

floggin' oggies
and bara brith

cynically palming
the Queen's shilling

resenting the till's
Quisling ring

Kerching
        Kerching
                Kerching

Goronwy ap Dewi
Llys Y Wennol,
Yr Hen Berllan,
Lon Ty Gwyn,
Cwm Penmachno,
Conwy.

22nd June 2004

Professor John Glyn,
Department of History,
The University of Wales,
Bangor.

Dear Professor Glyn,

I write in response to your letter seeking information pertaining to the direct action taken by Nationalist elements in Wales during the 1980's and early 1990's; I hope that the following will be of some use to your research.

When I was a child at home there was an awareness that we were Welsh and that our culture was important, although I can't recall actually discussing it as a family. Our awareness of who we were probably came naturally from both parents who, although not deeply immersed in Welsh culture, had a keen sense of their history and a republican, anti-royalist outlook.

My father had spent 18 years working in Argentina, so I suppose the mere fact that he returned to Wales after all that time hints at some kind of commitment or attachment to the country. Interestingly I found a reference from my father's boss in Argentina (himself a Welshman) expressing disappointment at his decision to return to Wales and hinting that his 'nationalism' wouldn't serve his career well and that it was time for "us Welshmen" to forget Gwalia Fach and make their lives in the New World.

I don't think as children we perceived the in-coming English as a threat to our culture and language. You don't feel these things until your teens or young adulthood. One was quite aware that many English people were moving in and had done for years. And, in retrospect, I can see that our generation was probably the first generation where the linguistic balance was finally tipped. Although most of my pals at home were Welsh speakers, there were, by then, enough homes where English was the first language for us to play at school through the medium of English.

Another indication of our awareness of the English language making in-roads was my father's angry admonishments if we used English at home 'Be iaith di honna da chin siarad?' 'What's that language that you're speaking?'

By the time I was a young man the notion of direct action was very much in the news; civil rights marches in Derry and Belfast for example. I would say that the furore over the Tryweryn business was the spark that ignited my nationalist ardour.

The opportunity to actually take direct action took place with Cymdeithas Yr Iaith. Luckily, probably, for me and a number of my activist friends, Cymdeithas was a movement based strictly on non-violent principles. I remember hearing Saunders Lewis's lecture telling us that the language would be dead in 50 years if we did nothing.

So, we occupied holiday homes (other groups were responsible for the cottage burning policy), we removed road signs, climbed and chained ourselves to radio masts, broke into council buildings and tax offices and shredded and re-arranged files.

I was arrested on a number of occasions and eventually imprisoned for non-payment of fines.

I still feel that the action we took was necessary, effective and justified. To think that at the time a Welsh speaker had no right to use his own language in the courts of law, that it had no official status, still makes my blood boil. The campaign for Welsh road signs has been seen by many as a trivial one; however, seeing Dolgellau written as Dollgelly (and other even worse abominations) was an insult to Wales and the Welsh. Other members of the broad nationalist camp thought our protests ineffectual. Meibion Glyndwr orchestrated the arson campaign and although I didn't agree with their methods I could sympathise with their anger. In the end I believe it was on-going pressure from differing groups that enabled the language to be protected. The language is safer now and I believe that's as a direct result of the nationalist pressure put on Westminster.

I hope you find some of the above useful.

Please let me know if I can be of any further help.

Yours Sincerely

Goronwy Ap Dewi

Nain and Taid come to tea
Ellesmere Port, 1967

tinned salmon
meat in jelly

salad in a big bowl
tea in small cups

(boiledegghalves)
prawns   sometimes

fruit cocktail
mandarins in syrup

CARNATION MILK;

in Dad's special chair
Taid's legs crossed

thick tweed trousers
thick woollen socks

polished brogues

Ink Spots racked
on the Dansett

Earth Angel
Earth Angel

A discordant cacophony

Nain's curse
guttural

*Duw, Duw, paid a fod
a cythraul fach.*

And Taid
Softly

Hush now woman,
leave the boy alone.

before Port Dinorwick
became Y Felinheli

on the backyard parapet
men of Harlech
with scouse accents
used volley fire
to decimate the Zulu
in the rhododendron

scanned the hill
with shielded eyes
for Mexicans

while Annie Pritch
wrung dry her best frock
at the mangle

polished the front step
for her prince

waved two flags
at his investiture

and years later
after the earthquake
when the battle was won

returned her post
to the council offices
in Caernarfon

because she couldn't read
their clever Welsh

FF. Gelynin. In the corner of Llangelynin churchyard: it's water taken for baptism. It was used for divination: clothes of sickly children were placed in the water; if they floated there would be a cure, if not, death would occur.

.....said to cure warts, lameness, blindness, scrofula, scurvy, rheumatism.....

.....used to divine a lovers intentions.....

(h) the goddess Gwenhudw

.....An eel living in it gave it much virtue.....

FF. Gwynwy. About a quarter of a mile from Llangelynin church: for the cure of warts a bent pin was dropped into the well *before* bathing: if this was not done, it was believed that, not only would the bathing be ineffective, but that the neglectful visitor would 'catch' the warts of which the previous ... the had got rid of. The prefix *Gwen* evidently represents an effort in Christian times to disguise the true origins of the goddess.

.....some money was left on the altei iui uic 'priestess': the water was lifted out by a limpet shell.....

.....surrounded by a stone seat enclosed within walls: there is a cromlech and megalith in its vicinity.....

.....lately a round vessel of black stone was found at its bottom, which was nearly full of pins.....

.....the water has tonic qualities and is said to steam in frost weather; its waters were especially good for weakly children and paralysed limbs.....

If the evidence of well names can be accepted, one goddess, Gwenhudw, has remained with Welshmen to modern times. She was originally a water deity, and the element.....*hudw (hudwy, hidwy, hidw)* in her name indicates a connection with primitive magic.

...and the American kept saying jeeze and wow because the clouds were alive the wind malevolent and the rain stung her face like flung gravel, the valley sunk under two feet of water, the black rap on the big bales ripped and torn bucked and billowed wild not unlike the hoods of monks or decadent friars, water bubbled from the ground, water poured out of the sodden earth, a crow or rook plucked from a branch and hurled at us, the American ducked and just kept saying oh my god oh my god, a crow flung like a black rag, like a shroud, right at us, there was a vague bluegrey steely impression of Siabod and two trees were down their medusa roots alive, still twitching, pools of water everywhere, bubbling up, even on top of the hill, bubbling geyser like and the American kept on saying jeeze, a little frightened by then, so we sheltered in the chamber with the witches and their small solstice offerings of hazel and hawthorn wrapped in cloth and the dark men with their whistles and coins, I showed her the names of the elder farmers carved in stone and a last sprig of Herb Robert clinging to an upright, but she didn't like it, I could see that, the way the wind sang an ancient song through the portal and tried to raise the capstone, she touched the mottled grey green lichen with her tongue, pressed her cold face against the stone and shivered, the dogs too, anxious, the setter pawing my legs and moving against my thigh, away from the crones, we stepped out onto the mound, stood hunched and humped, backs against the gale, the chamber beneath our feet thumbed into the earth, at sea, all at sea, the gorse flapping and cracking like a great yellow sail, the netting fence down, wrylock hung on skeletal fingers of weather worn oak the top wire loose and singing, bruised outline of Dafydd, Llewelyn and the whaleback ridges of the Carneddau, like hiking down a waterfall the road to the valley a flooded torrent and the American kept on saying jeeze and wow, the river the colour of tea, tannins and leafloamed earth carried from the hills to the sea, the river full, replete, an obese meandering, rolling, gouging the banks, carrying the hills to the sea, and the American kept saying wow...

[Pete the Poet my arse, who the fuck's 'e think 'e is eh, bit too big for his fuckin' boots if you ask me and fuckin' misogynistic or wot, I mean ain't he got fuck all to say about Welsh birds?]

trail

our

cuts

buzzard

the

wings

fingered

on

spiralling

vale

lazy

a

of

warmth

the

on

high

thermal

stolen

a

of

throat

the

in

caught

...see beautiful Gwenno's long black jackdaw hair and dark eyes deep as the dog lakes on Cnicht; see Gwenno's pale Snowdon lily skin shining white as death; see her full lips painted red as a dragon's tongue; see Gwenno in the square in Llanrwst tottering on heels higher than the mountain she lives on; see Gwenno's pot-bellied mid-rif exposed to sub-zero arctic conditions on the walk to parties in Penmachno; hear Gwenno's thunder thighs hissing under a skirt shorter than the name of her house on the hill; see Gwenno lobbing lambrini bottles into the middle of fights in Ffestiniog; pressing her breasts into the backs of boys on barstools in bars in Blaenau; see Gwenno and her valley commandos launching night-time assaults on Conwy quay; see Gwenno shooting tequila slammers in bistros in Bangor; leaning out of limos in Llangefni; French kissing squaddies in the backs of taxis in Tregarth; listen to Gwenno laugh and shriek and howl and dance a crazy ballet druidic in her ruin and prophetic as a skunked dervish in clubs in Caernarfon; see wild Gwenno scaring all and sundry shitless in pubs in Pwllheli...

Mach 1
and 100ft

over Nant Peris

the bouldered floor
of the pass
a papier mache blur

bank west

into the Ogwen
heather and gorse
a merged impression

in a Tornado
full of testosterone
and expletives

Pilot Officer Dai Morgan
from Swansea [*Mumbles*]
South Wales

and

Navigator Idris Jones
from Penmachno [*Cwm*]
North Wales

bomb a bus
on the Bangor Road

plot a course to Puffin Island

argue loudly
about who is the most Welsh

Llangelynnin

that last walk
we all joked
a little too hard
tried to ignore
the way the pain
in your back
made you bend
into the hill;
it was warm
stone walls
sectioned Tal Y Fan
a meadowlark
sang above Caer Bach;
in the corner
of the churchyard
the holy well,
you laughed
said anything
was worth a try,
but we didn't
and now
I wish we had
I wish I'd
bathed your neck
your back
wish I'd held you
softly
in the water
gently
like I did once
when we were young

On composite principalities:

...when states are acquired in a province differing in language, in customs and in institutions, then difficulties arise; and to hold onto them one must be very fortunate and very assiduous. One of the best, most effective expedients would be for the conqueror to go to live there in person...

the other superior expedient is to establish settlements... settlements do not cost much and the prince can found them at little or no personal expense...he injures only those from whom he takes land and houses to give to the new inhabitants...

on a bootlace of black-top
a Sherpa perambulates

stops

a learner boards
tries to purchase a ticket

to Pen Y Pass

in faltering Wlpan Welsh

the conductor stares back
blankly
feigns ignorance
shrugs, twice,

has her say it again in English

at her stop
he stops her

listen Cariad

he says in a slow sing-song
Caernarfonshire Cymraeg

it's nothing personal
but leave us something eh Del
leave us our language

to kill and skin and paunch and pluck
to pull and heal and sheer and trim
to box a bullock
to fence
to live well off the hard land;

against the hill
against the wind
against the grey slope of the yard
against the slanted drizzle
the farrier leaned
against the pony's slick belly
feathered hoof in a cupped hand
whispering *paid paid Cariad bach paid wan*
into her tipped ear;

a gentle man who fought like fuck
at the fairs, shows and pubs
of his roving country life

and left a twinkle in the eye
of many a wild haired child of the valley

and always whistled his coming
not wanting to impose
even though the favour was always his

and saw in the incomer's
ragwort pulling
gorse burning
love of well water
a kindred spirit
of hard graft
and commitment to the rough fields;

a prize fighter's stance
coal sack shoulders
hunched heavily
under a binder twined mantle
regal as ermine

and whose lump hammer hands
rabbit punched the fool
who sought the sun
while the breached ewe lay dying
alone in the coconut gorse
that first early spring lambing

his milk float coffin borne away
along the rowdy rounds of his youth

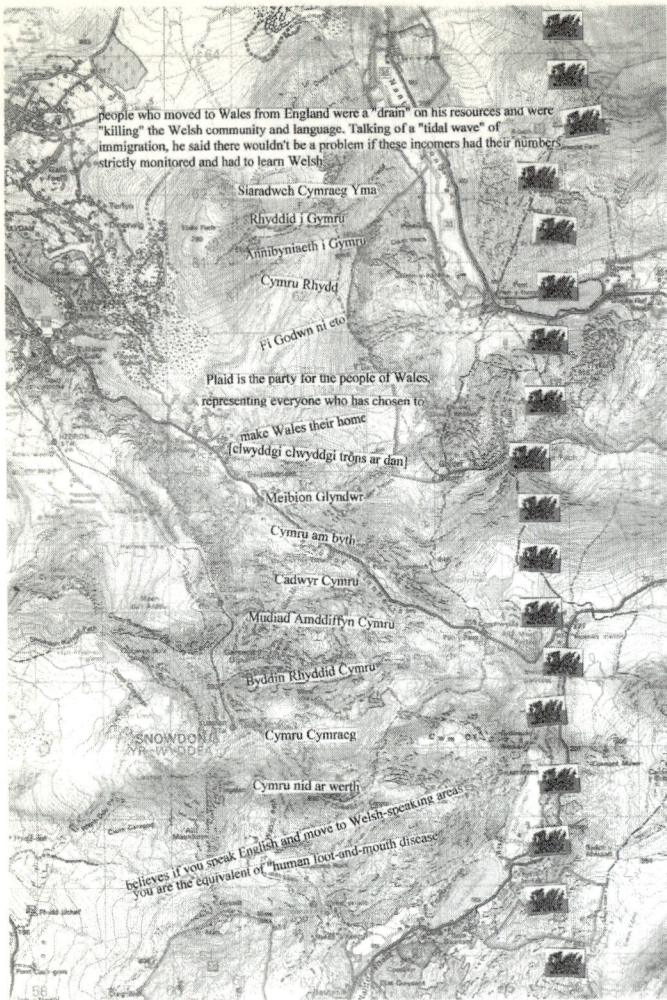

people who moved to Wales from England were a "drain" on his resources and were "killing" the Welsh community and language. Talking of a "tidal wave" of immigration, he said there wouldn't be a problem if these incomers had their numbers strictly monitored and had to learn Welsh

Siaradwch Cymraeg Yma

Rhyddid i Gymru

Annibyniaeth i Gymru

Cymru Rhydd

Fi Godwn ni eto

Plaid is the party for the people of Wales, representing everyone who has chosen to make Wales their home
[clwyddgi clwyddgi trôns ar dan]

Meibion Glyndwr

Cymru am byth

Cadwyr Cymru

Mudiad Amddiffyn Cymru

Byddin Rhyddid Cymru

Cymru Cymraeg

Cymru nid ar werth

believes if you speak English and move to Welsh-speaking areas you are the equivalent of "human foot-and-mouth disease"

...I'll tell you what ol' son
'ere's one you ain't goin' to fuckin' Adam 'n' Eve

the Driptrays are off on a beano up to Wales, mob-handed
they were, usual suspects, they've watched England total
the Taffs at the Arms Park and then they've hit the piss in
Cardiff, down Queen Street, and it's fuckin' chocker, loadsa
banter but no grief, you know how it is, shed loads of Skull
Attack and spurious trough down Mary Street, monkey
kebabs, giant purple onion bajis the fuckin' works, anyway

cut a long story short

next morning they ain't lost no one and they've taken Dry
Dave and Borin' Norman as a coupla designated so feelin'
rough as fuck they all crash in the back of the mini-van
callin' for sundry fuckin' puke and piss stops and after five
hours of purgatory end up in North Wales in some fuckin'
Taff town called BetWusWhyCood or some such shite
where Fatty Belly Frosty's booked 'em a gaff, anyway

cut a long story short

the drum's run by this geezer from Billericay who's a real
diamond and duz 'em a discount so it's all looking fuckin'
cushdy until the next day when they decide to have a
cabby around the manor to see what's occurrin', now as
you very well know the boys ain't fuckin' Philistines are
they and Fatty Belly's told me the scenery up there was
pukkah, anyway

cut a long story short

suffice to say he's banged on about how the mountains and
wot not were strictly the dog's bollocks, even Suicidal Jez's
got moony about it and you know what a grim fuckin' twat
he is, but, says Fatty Belly, and 'ere's the thing, 'e reckons
'e's never met such a bunch of fuckin' surly miserable
bastards in his life as the trogs what dwell up in them thar
hills

he reckons it must be the weather or summit in the bleedin' water but every pub or shop or garage they go into they get fuckin' blanked, the locals all cop a deaf un, or, and this is worse, they start talking fuckin' Welsh amongst themselves the rude bastards, and, get this, they've painted English Go Home or English Out all over the shop too, anyway

cut a long story short

all the road signs have either been fuckin' nicked or fuckin' turned around the wrong way so the boys ain't got a clue where they're at and end up in some fuckin' pikey shite hole called Lambworst or some such bollocks where, pissed off and fuckin' thirsty, they've decided, against Borin' Norman's expressed advice, to get rat arsed, anyway

cut a long story short

they hear this fuckin' jinky jink music comin' from this one boozer and make a bee line for it, Big Nose, followed by Sweets, is first through the door and straight up he tells me it's gone deathly, a real fuckin' deliverance moment, every Taff in the place has turned to stare at our boys who, as one, think fuck you lot and head for the bar, order up and start drinking, anyway

cut a long story short

things settle down until Suicidal Jez backs into this old geezer sittin' by himself at the bar and spills his drink, course 'e does the honourable, holds his hands up and tells the old scrote sorry granddad I'll get you another thinking that'll be that, but the old fucker ain't 'avin' it and tells Suicidal not to call him granddad and stands up fists clenched, anyway

cut a long story short

there's this old geezer standin' there dressed in a coat made out of old fuckin' sacks, straight up, fuckin' sacks, tied up with orange string, so Jez has told him leave it out granddad and fuckin' wallop the old bloke's hit him, just the once, and Suicidal goes down like a sack of hammers coughin' blood and wheezin' like he's goin' to puke a rib, anyway

cut a long story short

as one the boys step forward to help and the Taffs must have thought they're goin' for the old fella who's just standin' there smilin' like 'e's at a fuckin' wedding and course all hell breaks loose, every Taff in the place wades in, by all accounts it's like Dodge fuckin' City in there, even the Taffy tart's are chuckin' fuckin' empty Lambrini bottles into the ruck, anyway

cut a long story short

as you very well know some of the Driptrays are pretty handy themselves but they've all told me it was like fighting a bunch of fuckin' savages, fuckin' monsters they were, Big Nose is twattin' this one Taff over and over in the mush and he just keeps on walking forward and smiling, and when he does swing for Big Nose it's like he's been hit with a fuckin' fence post still he cracks on and

the boys cop hold of Suicidal and fight a fuckin' rear guard action to the door the last thing they see as they get outside is Little Legs bein' held up at arm's length by some giant fuckin' Taff, Legs is swingin' round house punches and hitting fuck all but air, 'course the boys ain't got time to worry about Legs because they're bein' chased up and down the main drag by hordes of fuckin' Genghis like Taffs, anyway

cut a long story short

53

they fight their way to the van and beat a hasty back to the hotel lickin' their wounds and, frankly, not givin' much of a fuck about Little Leg's predicament, because none of 'em fancy going back to get another fuckin' good hidin,' turns out the Taff's have taken Legs prisoner and have got a couple of huge Taffy tarts to keep an eye on him, now 'e ain't my cuppa tea but this one Taff bird called Gwenno takes a bit of a fuckin' shine to Legs, ticklin' his tummy, touslin' his hair and whispering sweet nothings in Welsh in his shell like, but when the Taff lads get back from chasin' our boys all over fuckin' Snowdonia he thinks he's gonna get a good hidin' but no, they ask his name and he tells 'em, David Parry he says, which is fuckin' news to yours truly because I could have sworn his name was Mr. Legs, anyway

cut a long story short

turns out there's a whole fuckin' tribe of Parrys up there and he's welcomed as a long lost brother who, they say, is goin' to have to learn the Welsh national anfem, in Welsh, as a punishment for fraternising with the English, course up until then Legs has always sung Whales Whales fuckin' great fishes are Whales but he's banged to rights and does his best, anyway

cut a long story short

takes 'em 12 fuckin' hours to teach him the first verse, then the local plod turn up and Legs thinks thank fuck for that I'm off, but the Taff girlies tell the old bill what's occurred and they only insist on teaching Legs the second verse, eventually he gets it and the Taffs take him to the local station, buy him a ticket back to Essex and after a tearful farewell send him on his way, anyway

cut a long story short

the whole experience has turned the poor little fucker, 'e don't go to Marbella no more, does 'e fuck, he takes 'is 'ols up in Lamb fuckin' Wurst, and, so Fatty Belly tells me, 'e only started singin' the wrong fuckin' anfem at Twickers, and, fuckin' stranger still, on my life, 'e only goes an' marries that Gwenno sort, and I'll tell you somefink for nuffink my old china,

if that ain't some sorta fuckin' fable my arse ain't got a fuckin' 'ole in it.....

[sic]

I use one ancient ritual for cleansing and exercising negativity from a damaged aura. I swallow a small frog (rain spirit of purification) and then, while the frog's spirit is alive inside me, I take holy water into my mouth and spay the client's aura.

I use old crow bones for divination.

I have stones placed in an around my home for their medicine and use them to make charms.

Nant Peris

it's mine dark
in the middle
of the day
and in the ruined barn
chained collies howl
so many shades of grey
boned and quarried crag
rain-sky-scree-slag
a stunted chimney
a twist of smoke
the squat church
slate headstones
slumped angular
askew
like busted teeth
in a quarryman's gob
and there
amidst the dank
boneyard dereliction
and decay
between two yews
in a swirl
of drizzled mist
his obelisk shines

1
Stan Taylor

She came up the stairs and said, 'Have you wet the bed?' I said, 'No, I haven't.' She said, 'You have and for that and for lying and being naughty and crying all the time for your mother, I'll put the dog in your bed and you'll go to the dog's place.' She brought up the collie dog and took off his collar and put it around my neck and put the dog in the bed. She put the chain around my neck, then she got the lead and dragged me down the stairs on my bottom...it was cold and wet and windy when she took me out to the back. I remember a black hole which was the dog kennel and being pushed into it and chained. I was left there all night screaming and crying. She done that every time I wet the bed. I hated it. And I hated them. And every night in my prayers I'd say, 'Oh dear God, please don't let me wet the bed again.'

2
Jimmy Callaghan

I returned to Liverpool back to the existence that I had left...bugs, fleas, lice and rats...isn't it amazing how quickly children adapt. I did. Bethesda remains my nirvana. I have never forgotten that idyllic period of my childhood. Every year I revisit my memories...my children and grandchildren have all grown up with North Wales firmly implanted in their souls, I have marvellous memories of Wales and the Welsh people, I'm still in touch with the family of the folks who gave me a home. The Welsh people could not have been kinder. My heart still very much belongs to Wales.

Legend has it that when Morwenna imprisoned Myrddin in a cave behind Moel Hebog there sat in the gloom at the back of the grotto a native hill farmer eating his lunch of sheep eyes and brains. It is said that Myrddin, desperate after a while for human discourse, sought to entertain the man with simple enchantments, tricks of the light, stories, songs and poetry; that he waited centuries for the farmer to comment, to smile, to make, perhaps, a witty quip, all to no avail. And it is told that when, millennia later, Glyndwr released the wizard by tapping the stone with his broad sword and asking for help the farmer spoke first, pushing himself forward to ask the would be king, with passion, and a glint in his eye, the price of spring lamb at the markets of Denbigh and the cost of feed in the stores of Llanrwst.

[*Trad, Anon.*]

a debate initially sedate

the poet speaks

personally I feel that an influx of diverse peoples enhances a culture and saves it from stagnation

in The Prince Llewelyn amber cwrw in chiselled pint pots

the bard reaches into his waxed jacket pocket, takes out a folded sheet of paper, and reads to bemused drinkers

> **Rhododendron** Rhododendron ponticum;
>
> In Snowdonia and other parts of the western British Isles, Rhododendron is a spectacularly invasive plant. From the bushes planted around a century ago in large gardens as pheasant cover, it has spread to occupy over two thousand hectares in Snowdonia alone. This has very negative consequences for wildlife. The bushes which can grow 3m or more have dense evergreen foliage. Very few plants can survive under the dense shade and the existing native vegetation is largely eliminated. Rhododendron itself is a poor substitute. The foliage is poisonous to most invertebrates and mammals and so does not support an extensive food chain. Its poisonous nature is one quality that makes Rhododendron so invasive, but it has several other strategies for survival. Bushes are long-lived; when they do eventually collapse, the branches layer and establish new plants. But the reason why Rhododendron is such an effective coloniser is the vast number of seeds it produces. A single large bush can produce one million tiny seeds per year. The seed needs special moist conditions to germinate successfully but even if only a single seed a year from each bush successfully became established, the invasion rate would be enormous. Most seeds land close to the parent plant and the invasion is most prolific at the edges of existing stands. However, in strong winds some seeds are carried much further, even several kilometres.

the lad serves

a bottle of finest Penderyn

waving a gnarly hand at the hills outside, swaying slightly, the bard stares into the blank faces of tourists and locals alike and goes on

esgob fawr a'i gathod fach boy, it's a fuckin' methaphor lad, a metaphor for the English plague, for the colonisation of our country lad, Rhod-o-fuckin'-den-dron boy, don't you see, it's the fuckin' Saes isn't it

the bard stands, steps forward, misses the step, performs an ungainly pirouette into a pub table full of holiday makers and freshly cut sandwiches

the lad enquires as to his well-being

the bard concludes

naar boy I'm fuckin' drunk as fuck, is there any more whiskey lad, and don't go...

Beech Plantation Rowen

equidistant, uniform, lopped;
mottled duck-egg bark,
wrought canopy, woven carpet,
almost too much wealth;
a surfeit of goldleaf
and the gaudy light
gleaming uncanny,
iconic,
through an opaque
gauze of mist;
tendrils of ivy climb,
knotted whale eyes blink and
hipposkinned lips on trunks
swallow the arrowed signs;
the path,
leaflittered beechmast,
mud and moss,
trails chainish through
the quarried wood;
in the breeze
each perfectly crafted leaf
falls, tumbles, spirals,
describes
an individual journey home

I know that well water still maintains its powerful healing properties and have witnessed on many occasions a rapid and powerful healing from the use of well water when conventional medicine has failed.

I treated a girl with anaemia following a large blood loss during the birth of her first child. The anaemia had led to further illness in her inner being and she felt lost and in utter despair. She had been prescribed double doses of iron and had had iron injections with no effect. The medical team wanted to re-admit her for a blood transfusion. My father and I took her to Ffynnon Ty Nant on the moor above Ysybty Ifan, we bathed her and prayed to the water deity and the girl drank the water we offered her. Two days after ingesting the water the girl felt better on all levels and five days later her midwife was shocked, but thrilled, to see that her blood iron levels were almost back to normal.

Of course it could be argued that the mineral content of the well water produced the cure, but the healing went much deeper than the physical; her emotional, mental and spiritual bodies felt vibrant and rejuvenated almost instantaneously. The girl's strength and smile and good humour returned almost at once; what better gift could the earth mother bestow upon her child, herself a new mother?

curl of woodsmoke
outside

and inside

scent of rosewood
and sage

patchouli

in the inglenook

crackle of pine

a little wenlock
thrums

hearthstones
radiates

warmth

oakwood and ash logs
are stacked

by a scuttle of anthracite

and baskets of scavenged
hazel tinder

little Gwenno
helps Hen Taid
with his Cynghanneth

slender harpist's fingers
tap tap tap tap
the strict metrical rhythm

a single blue vein
pulsing hieroglyphic
under her bwrw eira brow

causes consternation
by exclaiming her wish
to join the English stream

with her pals
when she goes up
to the big school next year

Letter sent to Prime Minister by President of Plaid Cymru (Welsh Nationalist Party), Alderman Gwynfor Evans, MA., Ll.B.,

July 28th 1957

"The Tryweryn issue has been widely understood in Wales to be crucial for the future of the national language and way of life. Therefore the Third Reading on Wednesday of Liverpool Corporation's Bill to drown the Valley is a fateful occasion for Wales.

No national issue during this century has united the Welsh people as strongly as this. Over a long period their will has been clearly and forcefully expressed by hundreds of representative assemblies. The biggest cities in England have seen Welsh men, women and children from Cwm Tryweryn pleading for the right to live in their homes undisturbed, and in the Bill's Second Reading not a single Welsh M.P. gave it support. There can be no doubt about the conviction of Wales in the matter. Wales stand firm in the defence of its heritage.

Liverpool Corporation demands a huge quantity of water from Merioneth, not because its reasonable needs cannot be met elsewhere – there are a dozen possible sources in England – but because Cwm Tryweryn is the cheapest and most profitable source to exploit.

In these circumstances to force the Bill through Parliament by an English majority, with the incongruous help of the Minister for Welsh affairs, can do no more than give a veneer of legality to an immoral act of aggression. It would be a declaration by the English majority in Parliament that it has the power to destroy Wales and will not refuse to do so if it thinks this would be in the interests of a part of England.

Liverpool will have enlisted the power of the strong to force the weak into submission, and its success may soon be emulated by other corporations and bodies who will have observed how powerless Wales is to protect her community and resources.

If we Welshmen accepted this passively, it would be a betrayal on our part. If all legal and constitutional endeavour to defend the Welsh heritage is ignored despite the unity and depth of Welsh conviction, the defence must continue, but by other means."

Regards,
Goronwy ap Dewi

A medicine sister uses magic water from a sacred well. She wears a tiny vial hung on a silver chain around her neck; she uses the water for divination and as a tool to douse clients, their homes, surroundings and to ascertain treatments.

...at the Urdd Eisteddfod frantic teachers panic like flushed quail, herd their flocked charges to and from the podium, bemused incomers view the same skits over and over and over again, watch their children sing songs and recite poems with pained expressions on their gurning faces like little angels with belly ache, and at the back of the hall Tazzer, from Toxteth, importer of exotic flowers, drug dealer and sometime paratrooper is wired into his I-Pod watching the man on the door holding it shut with a piece of binder twine, the man will not let anybody in or out of the hall, not while there's a performance on, it is more than his job is worth, he shakes his head impassively at the little girl who desperately needs the toilet, Tazzer keeps watching, watches the man's cold stare, watches him raise a finger to his lips to hush the little girl who is pleading with him to be let out, watches as the child clutches herself but cannot stop the urine from running down her legs, Tazzer, perhaps mistaking culture for cruelty and tradition for torture bides his time, follows the man along school corridors lined with dragon art and daffodils to the toilets, nuts him into the cubicle [*shattered probiscus spraying snot, blood and gore*] takes out his cock and sprays a frothy stream of Jagermeister and Red Bull inspired piss over his sharply pressed moleskin trousers, leans forward to admonish the chap, Ow d'you fuckin' like it eh lah, ow do you fuckin' like it you fuckin' nasty fuckin' nazi bastard, culture is it eh lah, I'll give you fuckin' culture...

frontiersville
the wild west

townsfolk
mountain men
trappers, hunters,
homesteaders with
violent cabin fever

all out for blood

searching for squaws
and scalps

los indios

tribal affiliations
blood feuds

there are no piazzas
here
no marbled plaza
no early evening
promenade
chic Champs Elysee
tables
bob in the Seiont

hey gringo
you non fron roun here

in this place all stakes
are claimed
this land
is most definitely not
up for grabs

come to hunt the aborigines
eh pilgrim, well
ye'll find 'em right lively

Caernarfon
world heritage site
Dodge fuckin' City
on a Saturday night

[The causes of the plague were] thickness of inhabitants; those living as many families in a house; living in cellars; want of fitting accommodations, as good fires, good dyett, washing, want of good conveyances of filth; standing and stinking waters; dung hills, excrements, dead bodies lying unburied and putrefying; churchyards too full crammed; unseasonable weather ...

The Diseases and Casualties this year

Yersinia pestis bacillus

bubonic

septicaemic

pneumonic

[highly contagious especially in crowded poorly ventilated buildings]

chancres

buboes

rodent ulcers

beyond Maelgwyn's ruined halls
the Vardre falls away
into once fertile coastal plains
where sceptic tanks
ooze human slurry
and a spider cancer
rash
of corrugated petri boxes
appals

70

after the cut
round bales
    sag
      pregnant
into womby
    earth
    cast
random shadows
    upon
moleskin farmers
    whose
chequerbellies
    bulge
belted and braced
against the gate
of the farm
at their
dealerbooted feet
supine collies
    whimper
while the lurcher

Fizz

twitches, wired
paws the soil
slips the leash
a kinetic blur
    contoured
against the
falling meadow
and in the wetter
    bottomland
fallow bunnies
    bolt

I am a direct descendant of the bonesetters of Anglesey; medicine men and women who used spells, incantations, lotions and potions to set bones and heal skeletal problems.

My father always treated us kids himself when we were sick with herbs and "old wives tale" remedies which never failed to work. His herb garden remains a thing of beauty. He has a great knowledge of nearly all plant medicine. He recently removed several large and unsightly warts (which had not responded to conventional treatment) from the chest, neck and back of a teenage girl using a potion made from the sap of Greater Celandine (Llysiau'r Wennol.)

My maternal grandmother was a medicine woman (even though she was also the organist at the village chapel.) She used traditional cures on all her 13 children and could read the book of nature, knowing what the clouds said, or the leaves, or the way animal behaviour could predict events, or birds' movements could tell of potential health problems. She held séances once a month. Most of her clients attended the staunchly Methodist chapel three times on Sundays. When they visited her they'd come in over the fields and enter through the back door.

Pen y Gaer
ring fort

concentric circles
within circles

stone and earth
embankments

chevaux de frise

round huts

and in the valley
north of Tal y Cafn

the legion crossed

in phalanxed centuries
and columns

caerhun camp

squared, angular,
bedded in by degrees

incompatible
geometries

square pegs
round holes

at the wall's
reticulated curve
Ned
Iwan
Charlie
Cae
Joe
and Llewelyn
rap in a
pigeon patois
of Welsh
and English
remember
the mason's creed
make the stones
fit the wall

[...Pete the fuckin' Poet my arse, I mean who the fuck does
'e think 'e's fuckin' kiddin' and why's 'e always bangin' on
about Welsh fuckin' water for Christ's sake, I mean

      it's

          all

              the

                    fuckin'

                          same

                                ain't

              it

and why's 'e keep on repeatin' hisself eh, like a fuckin' tap
'e is, on and fuckin' on,

      drip

          drip

              fuckin'

                  drip...]

the view lies
somewhere beyond
the drizzle

in the stone built shelter

droplets of water condense

on the underside
of the Vaynol slate roof

a cist of granite uprights
set into soft earth

slate black water

almost frozen
slow, viscous,
touched latex

[a neoprene print]

and oiled, mineralish,
rubbed between
thumb and forefinger

droplets of water condense

reluctant
          pendulous

in here
water speaks

echoes itself

an oral tradition
endlessly

repeated

outside
on the old drovers' road

things pass and change

under the lake
the waterfalls
the streams

flowing
sunlight

three boys
small fry

bamboo fishing
for minnows

toes in silt
sunlight on water
flat black stone

skimming
the bridge
the moor

tiers

here and now
there and then

everything
everything

floating away